Auntie Seagu...

Potato Basics......

a potpourri of recipes,
how to and spud lore

from Prince Edward Island

by Julie V. Watson

Seacroft

Copyright 2010 Julie V. Watson
First edition
First printing

Cover design & production facilitator: Pollywog Desktop Designs
Writing, design & layout: Julie V. Watson

Published by:
    Seacroft
    P.O. Box 1204
    Charlottetown
    Prince Edward Island
    Canada   C1A 7M8
    Email: biz@seacroftpei.com
    Web: www.seacroftpei.com

Library and Archives Canada Cataloguing in Publication

Watson, Julie V., 1943-
Auntie Seagull's Potato Basics......a potpourri of recipes, how to and spud lore from Prince Edward Island

Includes index.
ISBN 978-0-9865489-0-1

Prince Edward Island, potato cookbook, potatoes, history

TABLE OF CONTENTS

INTRODUCTION 4
    Introducing Auntie Seagull 5
    History 6

GENERAL INFORMATION 7
    Storage 9
    Preparation 10

COOKING UP PERFECT POTATOES 11

OVEN COOKING 12
    Baking 12
    Roasting 15
    Casseroles and Scalloped 18
    Pies 20

ON THE STOVE TOP 22
    Boil 'Em 22
    Steaming 24
    Mashing 24
    Skillet Meals 27
    Frying 29
    French Fries 32
    Soups and Chowders 34

OTHER STUFF 37
    Salads 37
    Breads and Sweet Treats 40

BOOKSTORE 46

INTRODUCTION

Within months of arriving in Prince Edward Island we moved into a sort of dream home. I say sort of because our dream was to have a small farm. What we got was a run down farmhouse, a couple of acres of land and no outbuildings. Three sides of our acreage were bordered by potato fields, a fact we alternately cursed and blessed.

The cursing came in spring when dust from farm equipment coated everything inside and out with clay-red grit. It came in summer and early fall when sprays drifted over our acres and forced us to keep horses, dogs and kids inside until it rained.

The blessing came in late fall, after the harvest. That was when neighbours with a basket and strong back could go on the field and scrounge spuds that had fallen off trucks, or been missed by diggers. We were assured that we could gather what we needed for our own use, as long as we got them before they froze. Since illness and unemployment meant we had no money those potatoes were lifesavers. We had days they were main course and snacks.

Winter was a mixed blessing. True we had enough spuds in our basement to ward off the hungries until spring. However our fences were perfect snow catchers. That snow, ground-drifting across the open potato fields until it hit these obstacles, filled our driveway with drifts that regularly hit 6 feet in depth, and on one memorable occasion were as high as the power poles.

Often referred to as poor man's fertilizer, snow and cold are said to be important to Prince Edward Island's top harvest. Whether due to long, cold winters and heavy snow coverage, quality of the soil, farming practices or just plain good luck, it is a reality that the province earned its moniker, Spud Island, by providing the world with quality seed and eating potatoes.

Potatoes have long been important and are always found in my pantry. In countries like my homeland, England, potatoes are part of traditional meals like Bangers and Mash or Shepherd's Pie. A favourite from childhood, Egg 'n' Chips, still tops my list of comfort foods. Made-from-scratch chips (or French Fries) served up with malt vinegar were our munchies.

Here in Prince Edward Island traditional potato dishes include chowder, fish-cakes, boiled dinner and stews, and the perennial favourite roast meat or poultry which usually seems to be served with mash potatoes, turnips and carrots. Potatoes "stretched" other ingredients for a fulfilling meal.

INTRODUCING AUNTIE SEAGULL

In a moment of frivolity, we decided we need a voice and created Auntie Seagull. As author, Julie V. Watson, and designer Helen Grant, we put this book together, but it is the wisdom of those who have been our teachers, our mentors, that make this information invaluable for the home cook.

Who is Auntie Seagull? The answer is that she represents many individuals met as part of our own lives, or through research and interviews. Auntie is a wise old bird. Her eyes aren't what they used to be, and her seashell jewelry might seem tacky to some, but she has seagull smarts and seagull wit.

Auntie remembers how to prepare food from scratch. She knows how to make nourishing, and satisfying, meals with basic ingredients. Most importantly she likes to share her knowledge and hopes that everyone learns the joy of serving up their best efforts without breaking the bank, slaving for hours, or relying on foods that have traveled for thousands of miles to get to our kitchens. Auntie believes in the locavor* concept. She's been a neat chick since she hatched!!   * *locavors are dedicated to freshly harvested local foods*

Who visits potato fields more than the farmer growing the crop? Why Auntie Seagull of course. She is there checking the soil as the land is turned. From her sky high view she keeps an eye on things all summer and is right there following along behind the potato harvester in the fall. Of course she is not the connoisseur of potatoes that we humans are. We have the smarts to turn this tuber into delicious dishes to tempt all palates.

As creators of this book we have one hope, that this information helps you to utilize this wonderful food to its highest potential, and enjoy the process to the fullest.

Julie and Helen

HISTORY

Having a bit of a fascination for the history of food I often wonder what it was that made the first human actually taste something. Imagine people of South America more than five thousand years ago. Foraging for food they must have come across a brown, rough little root, or stone-like thing attached to a root. What ever made them eat it?

Doesn't matter. They cultivated an incredible array of tubers which we collectively call potatoes. They came in a multitude of colours, flavours and textures: white, purple, blue, black, orange, pink, green, and of course brown. Shapes too were varied. Today we call them fingerlings, rounds, longs and producers and chefs often proudly announce "new" variations to patrons. Kind of ironic that these new "discoveries" of today actually existed some 5,000 years ago. An important food source to the Inca they revered them so much they became objects of worship.

Thus it was inevitable that the Europeans who invaded the world of the Andes would take some of these treasured potatoes back home. Exotic plants and new foods and flavours were favourite things for early explorers to take back to those who funded their jaunts to the New World.

There are many versions of who took potatoes to Europe, and eventually to North America, but it is pretty certain the Spaniards were first.

Eventually hunger drove acceptance of potatoes. France, Prussia, then a century or so later the rest of Europe came to appreciate them. There is a tale that one chef served the leaves, instead of the tuber to Queen Elizabeth I, an error that set back England's acceptance of spuds for hundreds of years.

The Irish, in particular, became very reliant on spuds (a name which came from the Gaelic for the spades or shovels used to harvest them). Irish soil and climate particularly suited potatoes which grew in abundance until the 1840s when a blight attacked crops and over a million people starved to death.

When Europeans settled North America the potato was a natural for pioneers to bring with them. Prince Edward Island, New Brunswick and later, points west, proved to have the soil and climate perfectly suited to raise superior potatoes which are now shipped around the world as well as being a staple in local homes.

Auntie Seagull talks about

General Information

Potatoes that you are buying in stores today have been graded, or basically sorted by type (long or round) and size. Most cooks have an idea of what potatoes they prefer: reds, yellows, bakers, baby size, etc. We usually visually check potatoes for the type and size we want. We pay attention to the variety, buying those which we found suited our taste on previous occasions. Even so, there are many more options out there than most of us consider. In our household local, and preferably organic, is our first criteria. We can be lured away from those ideals when something new and interesting presents itself and can be even more excited when a heritage spud surfaces.

Auntie says:

Many a Maritimer associates home with Blue Potatoes and when given a few will go into almost the same state of ecstacy as when an Islander land-locked in Upper Canada is presented with fresh lobster. Today most Blues are offered at farmers markets. Cooked in their skins they have a distinctive taste. Blues were often used with salt fish. One recipe for cooking them read, "Fill a large pot with potatoes in their jackets, add a handful of coarse salt and boil (after adding water we suppose). When they can be pierced with a fork take them to the back door and drain off water. Lift cover and give them three shakes in the wind."

Common PEI Potato varieties include:

Long come in irregular shapes, and can have large eyes, but are still an excellent multi-purpose potatoes that can be baked, boiled, mashed, French fried and microwaved. Include several varieties of Russets (aka Idahos in the USA): Burbank, Goldrush, Coastal, Norkotah. Shepody, also considered 'Long' potatoes, are not recommended for microwaving.

Round White have light, or white, skins and a cream or ivory coloured flesh. Waxy, these are a low-starch potato that boils well. They include Superior and Kennebec as well as Irish Cobbler varieties

Reds have characteristic red skin that is usually smooth, and white flesh. Also termed waxy they are an excellent potato for boiling, baking and mashing. Varieties include Chieftan, Norland and Red Pontiac.

Yellow, named for their yellow skin and flesh, are excellent multi-purpose potatoes. Known as Yukon Gold they have a firmness that many cooks favour, especially when used for slow cooking.

Shop at farmers markets, or farm gates and you might just luck into some of the traditional or novelty potatoes that chefs favour. Blues, have been around PEI for a long time - the flesh looks blue when raw, but usually turns white when cooked. Fingerlings or Lady Fingers are named for their size and shape. Purple and Black Potatoes have been experimented with, as have pinks.

If you find something different ask the producer for some recommendations about best ways to cook, then get brave and try some different spuds.

Auntie says:
When shopping look for clean potatoes free of dirt and with no blemishes, cuts or skin that doesn't look healthy. Remember that potatoes are not graded for cooking quality, so take note of which potatoes you and your family enjoy so that you can look for them next time.

Beware of Green

While many colours of potatoes are available there is one colour to be wary of - green. Green on the surface or through your potato is caused by exposure to the sun or bright light. It can occur on the farm, in the field by a potato poking up through the soil, in storage, or in your grocery store. Try not to buy green potatoes. If you do find some discard the "green" part of the potato - all of it. It can cause a burning sensation in your mouth or throat, upset your stomach or even cause headaches. And it often makes the potato taste bitter.

New Potatoes

True new potatoes are available from late spring through to fall. They are not just small, they are young. Be careful that you are not buying small potatoes vs new. The test is in the skin. New potatoes have thin skin which flakes easily when rubbed. They don't store as well as mature potatoes so use within a few days.

Auntie says:
Never store your potatoes in the fridge. Never! Ever!
The temperature causes the natural starch to turn to sugar.
This sugar can darken the flesh of the potato during cooking.

STORAGE

Store your potatoes at cool, not cold temperatures and keep them in the dark. Do not refrigerate them, but rather look for a cool, dry place. Beware of hot spots in your kitchen - the cupboard beside the stove or fridge can be too warm. Warmth can cause potatoes to sprout or shrivel up, or even get dry. Nutrients will be lost. A better place to store potatoes is the basement, a dark closet near an outside door - somewhere cool. Wooden potato bins are great but store potatoes alone. Sharing space with other veggies, especially onions, is not a good thing. Brown paper bags are better than plastic - ditch it when you get them home.

Handle potatoes with care. They do bruise and that can cause blackspot, broken or thickened skins. Remove any visible black spots before cooking.

FREEZE - OR NOT

Mashed, baked or stuffed potatoes freeze well, as do potato patties and French fries. Make sure all of the air is out of a plastic bag and use as soon as possible as freezer burn can be a problem. Cooked potatoes, other than above, do not freeze well, neither do those in soups or stews. Do not freeze raw potatoes.

HOLLOWHEART

A brown or blackened hole in the centre of a potato that looks perfectly normal on the outside is annoying, although it doesn't affect the taste or nutritional value. Caused by rapid growth, or unfavourable temperature changes it crops up with certain weather conditions, usually in larger potatoes. One way to ensure it doesn't get to the table, cut potatoes in half before cooking.

DARKENING SKIN

When peeling potatoes, immediately immerse them in cold water. They will turn dark on the outsid where cut, if left out in the air. Some say a little vinegar or lemon juice in the water keeps them from changing colour.

There are several other factors that can cause darkening to take place when cooking. Sometimes it is natural. If potatoes seem to darken during or after cooking try adding a little lemon juice to the water the next time you cook them. Also make sure you are not storing them in the refrigerator or too cold temperatures.

PREPARATION

Like all produce, potatoes should be washed before cooking. Use a soft vegetable brush to clean them under running water. Be gentle, the nutrients are in the skin which is a good reason to cook them without peeling. If you do decide to peel your potatoes, keep the peel as thin as you can to retain the nutritional value. Do remember to remove any green skin or flesh. The next step depends on how you plan to cook your potatoes.

Auntie says:
Don't store potatoes near apples. Apples give off a gas that will cause potatoes to sprout.

Auntie Seagull talks about

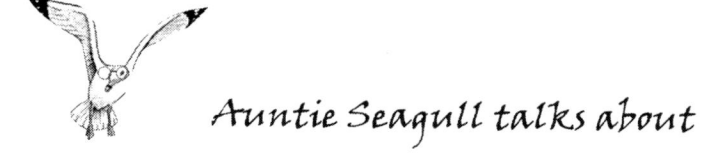

Cooking Up Perfect Potatoes

There so many ways to make perfect potatoes that it fair boggles the mind. Yet we tend to use a few simple basic methods; boiling, baking, and some form of frying, without taking the extra steps to make our potatoes a really pleasing addition to a meal.

In the following pages we help you explore ways to expand your potato repertoire. Most recipes are traditional, tried and true favourites. They come from folks we know as well as our own kitchens. They may well be reminders of things enjoyed in the past but forgotten in recent times.

They are a reminder that experienced cooks before us used potato to stretch more expensive or hard to come by ingredients. There was a time when a rural housewife had to treat flour, for example, with care because the trip to the mill was only made a few times a year.

Others will be totally new to you, a chance to experiment and have fun with this inexpensive main ingredient.

On the pages ahead we encourage you to spread your culinary wings and make the most of this inexpensive, readily available vegetable.

It isn't hard to do good things with potatoes as long as you have a heat source. It can be as old-time as a campfire, or as modern as a microwave.

Auntie Seagull talks about

Oven Cooking

Baking. Stuffing. Roasting

BAKING

Choose uniform sized potatoes for even baking. Pierce the skins of washed potatoes several times with a fork to allow steam to escape. Do not wrap in foil since this produces steamed, not baked potatoes.

Bake potatoes directly on the oven rack or baking sheet until for tender. Potatoes can be baked at different oven temperatures to accommodate other dishes in the meal. Use these times and temperatures as guidelines:

        425 degrees F / 220 C for 40-50 minutes
        375 degrees F / 190 C for 50-60 minutes
        325 degrees F / 160 C for 75-85 minutes

Auntie says:
Baking time can be decreased by inserting heated metal skewers or prongs through each potato. In days past cooks would shove a nail into one end of a potato to conduct heat to the inside and speed up cooking. Today we are a little more careful about what we use, so I suggest using skewers intended for making shish kabobs or a metal you know is safe. DO NOT use this method in the microwave.

BAKED POTATO ON THE SIDE
Sometimes you just want a plain baked potato to serve up with your meal. Bake followin guidelines below. Remove from the oven, make an "X" on one side by perforating with a fork or sharp knife. Fluff the potato flesh with a fork or "blossom" the potato by squeezing the ends toward the centre. Delicious with butter, sour cream or a dressing you have made.

Try making a topper using low-fat ranch dressing that has been spiffed up with the addition of chopped chives or green onion.

Auntie says:
To check baked potatoes for doneness, protect your hand with an oven mitt, then give your spud a squeeze. It will give when fully cooked.

STUFFED (TWICE BAKED) SPUDS
There is something satisfying about stuffed potatoes. Almost an ultimate comfort food they make us feel special because a little extra effort went into their preparation. There is also a huge benefit if you have fussy kids. Each individual potato can be unique in the added ingredients. I for example can't eat hot peppers. Husband and son love them. So I just leave them out of one and carefully note which is mine.

TEN STEPS TO A GREAT STUFFED POTATO
1. Start with a well-scrubbed baking potato for each person.
2. Preheat oven to 400F / 200C
3. Prick potatoes with a fork, lightly oil*, place on oven rack and bake for 45 minutes, or until tender
4. Hold potato lengthwise. Slice off the top about 1/4 of the way down
5. Scrape the pulp into a large bowl and discard the top skin.
6. Scoop out rest of the potato pulp, leaving a 1/4 in / 2.5 cm thick shell
7. Reduce the oven temperature to 350F/ 180C
8. Mash potato pulp, prepare stuffing and spoon into potato shells, mounding generously.
9. Place stuffed potatoes on a small cookie sheet.
10. Bake 15 minutes, or until heated through.

optional

The variety of stuffings is limited only by your imagination. Here are a few of our favourites

SAUSAGE AND CHEESE
Brown pork sausage (bulk or cut sausages) break into small pieces, drain well and add chopped parsley and the same amount of cheddar cheese. Combine with mashed potato and stuff into shells. Reheat in oven.

DECADENT STUFFED POTATOES
For each potato
  2 oz / 57 g cream cheese
  sprinkle snipped chives
  salt and pepper to taste
  paprika
  butter

Combine all ingredients except butter with pulp from potato, stuff. Dot butter on top and bake till heated through.

EVEN MORE DECADENT TWICE BAKED
These are so rich that half a potato is enough as a side dish.
  4 large baking potatoes prepared ready for stuffing
  1/4 cup / 50 mL butter or margarine
  1/4 cup / 50 mL whipping cream
  1 - 8 oz / 227 g carton sour cream
  3/4 cup / 175 mL sharp cheddar cheese, grated
  ½ cup / 125 mL green onions, chopped
  ½ tsp / 2 mL garlic salt
  1/4 tsp / 1 mL pepper
  1 oz / 28 g blue cheese, crumbled

Garnish:
  bacon, cooked to crisp and crumbled
  fresh chives, chopped

Mash pulp, butter and whipping cream until light and fluffy. Stir in sour cream, cheeses, green onions, garlic salt, and pepper. Spoon into potato shells and return to the oven to heat. Garnish and serve. Serves 8

VARIATIONS:
Go with your imagination when it comes to stuffing potatoes. Here are a few of our ideas. We urge you to take the things you like and experiment. Mash the potato pulp; sprinkle with salt and pepper and add:
* well drained crab meat, with cream cheese and cheddar garnish
* cottage cheese and chopped fresh herbs
* finely chopped mushrooms
* chopped lobster meat, grated cheese of choice, mayo
* finely chopped ham and minced scallions
* minced smoked salmon and snipped chives
* refried beans, shredded Monterey Jack cheese, & chopped green chilies
* chopped hard-cooked eggs, and minced herbs
* corned beef and diced red and green bell pepper
* steamed chopped mixed vegetables
* baby shrimp, condensed cream of shrimp soup
* chopped smoked chicken or turkey and minced tarragon
* drained flaked tuna and minced red onion
* chopped spinach and nutmeg
* chopped broccoli and grated cheddar cheese or cheese sauce

Auntie says:
It is said that to carry a piece of raw potato in ones pocket will ease the pain of rheumatism

ROASTING

One of the easiest way to cook potatoes is to roast them in the oven. Get it ready, toss it in and an hour or two later you have a great addition to a meal.

ROASTING WITH MEAT
There are few meals as comforting and delicious as traditional roast beef served with roast potatoes and rich beef gravy. Yum. Peel potatoes. Cut into quarters or halves if large. Arrange around meat in roasting pan, turning to coat with pan juices, 1 to 1 ½ hours before meat will be ready to serve. Cook at approximately 325 degrees F / 160 degrees C. Turn and baste with pan drippings at least once, preferably 2-3 times.

PAN ROASTING
Select the size for your pieces of potato based on the length of cooking time available. Place small whole, or pieces of potato, on parchment paper, in a shallow oven-proof pan. Drizzle or brush with olive or vegetable oil, rolling to coat all over. Sprinkle with lemon-pepper, aromatic herbs like rosemary, seasoning mix, paprika, chili powder or minced garlic if desired. Place in oven uncovered, and roast at 400 degree F / 200 degree C oven. Turn occasionally. After 45 minutes, test for doneness by poking with a fork. They should be fork tender between 45 minutes and one hour.

ROOT VEGGIE ROAST
Pan roasting works well for all root vegetables, producing delicious results. Potatoes, carrots, turnip, whole onions, etc., should be cut into similar size chunks and cooked as above. We also like to roast leeks and/or brussel sprouts with potatoes.

A TOUCH OF ENGLAND
Being British raised I've always cooked with a dash of Worcestershire in certain dishes. Roast veggies is one place where it shines, adding just a touch of different flavour. If you have a large group coming just increase quantities accordingly. This is a very forgiving recipe

6-8 potatoes, cut into quarters or thick slices
2 tbsp / 30 mL olive oil
1 ½ tsp / 7 mL Worcestershire sauce
1 tbsp / 15 mL butter melted
lemon pepper or other herb

Preheat oven to 400 F / 200C. Use a fork to blend oil and sauce, then add butter. Pour into a heated shallow baking disk, add potatoes and stir to coat in oil mixture. Sprinkle with lemon pepper or other herb mixture. Roast for 45 minutes, turning once. Potatoes are done when crispy on the outside, and soft when tested with a fork. Serves 4

Auntie says:
To make extra tasty topping for baked or mashed potatoes, roll butter balls in poppy seed, paprika, parsley or chives

Auntie says:

Worcestershire sauce is like a fine wine. Lea and Perrins age ingredients for more than three years. There is no way we housewives can duplicate the combination of onions, garlic, anchovies, shallots, malt vinegar, tamarinds, chillies, cloves, black strap molasses and "secret ingredients" that was created in 1837 as a sauce for aristocrats. Wise cooks take full advantages of prepared ingredients like soy sauce, Worcestershire and even tomato sauce or paste.

GARLIC POTATOES

By cutting a cross hatch pattern in the tops of potatoes you allow the flavours to penetrate, and provide a nice showy dish. You might like to sprinkle a little paprika, or other seasoning on before taking to the table.

> 1/4 cup / 50 mL garlic flavoured olive oil*
> 2 tbsp / 30 mL chopped fresh parsley
> 2 large or 4 medium baking potatoes
> 1/4 cup / 50 mL grated Romano or extra old cheddar cheese

Heat oven to 400F / 200C. Combine garlic flavoured olive oil and fresh parsley in a strong plastic bag. Season with salt if desired

Halve potatoes lengthwise. Using a sharp knife make criss-crossed cuts into the cut side of the potato, about ½ inch / 2 ½ cm deep. Toss potatoes in the plastic bag, reserving left over oil mixture. Place potatoes cut side down on baking sheet.

Bake until tender, about 30 minutes, depending on size of potatoes. Turn potatoes, then use a spoon or brush to add the remaining oil mixture, top each potato with grated cheese and return to the oven briefly to melt cheese. Serves 4

* *garlic flavoured olive oil can be purchased, or you can make your own by adding minced garlic to olive oil several hours before cooking.*

CASSEROLES AND SCALLOPS

POTATO TURNIP HORSERADISH CASSEROLE

1 1/4 cups / 300 mL whipping cream
2 lb / 1 kg russet potatoes, peeled, sliced thinly
1 1/4 cups / 300 mL turnip, peeled, halved, thinly sliced
1 1/4 cups / 300 mL half and half
1 tsp / 5 mL fresh rosemary, minced or ½ tsp / 2 mL dried rosemary
1/4 cup / 50 mL cream-style horseradish
salt and pepper to taste

Preheat oven to 400 F / 200 C. Lightly butter 8 inch / 20 cm square glass baking dish. Bring cream and half and half to boil in heavy pot over medium high heat. Add potatoes and turnips. Simmer about 5 minutes, until vegetables just begin to soften, stirring occasionally. Remove vegetables to baking dish. Add horseradish, rosemary, salt and pepper to cream, mix. Season with salt and pepper. Pour over vegetables. Press vegetables firmly to compact. Cover. Bake 40 minutes. Uncover and bake until vegetables are tender and top is brown, about 30 minutes longer. Let stand 10 minutes.
Serves 6-8

SWISS POTATOES

Bulletin! You don't need to cook potatoes with cream or milk. Stock works wonders. I love this preparation. Slice the potatoes into cold water to chill and prevent browning.

8 medium red potatoes, cut into thick slices and chilled in cold water
2-3 cups / 500-750 mL grated Swiss cheese
4 tbsp / 60 mL butter
1 cup / 250 mL chicken stock
salt and pepper

Preheat oven to 425F / 220C. Grease a 9x12 inch / 23 x 30 cm pan. Pat potatoes dry. Arrange half in dish. Sprinkle with salt and pepper, and half of the cheese. Dot with half of the butter. Repeat layer. Pour chicken stock over top. Bake 45-60 minutes or until potatoes are tender and top is golden.
Serves 6

FOOL PROOF CREAMY SCALLOPED POTATOES

This recipe works best if you mush the potatoes in the soup before combining with the milk. Its fool proof and creamier.

>   1 can Cream of Potato*soup
>   1 can milk
>   1 tsp / 5 mL salt, optional
>   pepper
>   6 potatoes, peeled and thinly sliced
>   a shake of dried onion or one medium onion, thinly sliced
>   grated Parmesan cheese
>   1 tbsp / 15 mL butter

Heat soup and milk. Add salt and pepper. Butter casserole dish and cover with a layer of potatoes. Pour some sauce over potatoes. Cover with a few onions. Repeat until ingredients are used up. Dot with butter. Sprinkle Parmesan over the top. Bake uncovered for 1 ½ hours at 350 F / 180 C or until potatoes are tender and top is golden. Serves 4
* *try varying the soup to another such as Cream of Celery*

SCALLOPED POTATOES

A much favoured way of serving potatoes, especially with ham. This recipe came to me some 35 years ago. It was still on an old envelop, as it had been passed down from the owner's grandmother.

"Melt 2 tablespoons butter, stir in 2 tablespoon flour. Add slowly 1 1/2 cups milk, stirring constantly. Cook and stir over low heat until thickened. Add 1/4 tsp salt and a dash of pepper. Remove from heat. In a buttered baking dish place 4 potatoes which have been peeled and sliced and onion, chopped fine. Pour the sauce over the top and bake in a 350 degree F oven for 1 1/4 hours or until potatoes are tender. Sprinkle buttered crumbs over the top before baking for a nice topping." Serves 4-6

Auntie says:
When slicing raw potatoes, for scalloped potatoes or chips, cut a small slice off one side to make a sturdy base.

PIES

PRINCE EDWARD ISLAND PRESERVE COMPANY POTATO PIE
Bruce MacNaughton, a great friend who ownes the Prince Edward Island Preserve Company and adjacent restaurant, gave us the recipe which is very popular in their New Glasgow eatery. Layers of fresh Prince Edward Island potatoes, Island cheddar cheese & chives baked in a bacon crust draw people back for repeats.

Thinly slice potatoes. Line a pie plate or casserole dish with bacon leaving half slice of bacon over the edge of dish. Layer potatoes, a generous amount of grated cheese, chopped chives, salt & pepper to taste. Repeat until you have four layers. (Sprinkle first layer only with ground thyme.) Pull bacon up over top. Pie should be 4-5 in. thick at middle. Fasten center with skewer. Bake at 350 F / 180 C for 2 hours.

SCOT'S PIES
Since Bruce is usually spotted wearing his kilt to greet visitors, it seemed appropriate to include a couple more Scottish "pie" recipes. Funnily enough these are baked in a potato, rather than in a pie dish.

Minced Meat Pie - Traditionally made with left over meat from a roast which was run through the meat grinder. You can substitute cooked ground beef, lamb or pork. Wash a large potato per person, holding it horizontally, slice off the top about 1/4 of the way down. Carefully remove the potato, using a paring knife, and leaving a ½ inch / 1 ½ cm shell. Parboil or fry a chopped onion. Mix the onion with enough meat to fill the potatoes, pepper, salt and leftover gravy. Stuff the potatoes with this mixture, put the tops back on and place in a greased baking dish. The original recipe says to baste often with dripping, but I just oil the outside of the potato once. Cook in a "quick" oven (400 degrees F / 200 C) for at least one hour. Serve with good rich gravy, or tomato sauce.

Angus Pie - prepare baked potatoes for stuffing (see page 13). Meanwhile prepare two cups / 500 mL of cooked, flaked Finnan Haddie. Remove potato pulp and mash, then add the smoked fish, with a little butter and milk to moisten. It should be creamy. Fill potato shells, piling high and return to the oven to heat through.

RÂPURE a.k.a. RAPPIE PIE

This traditional Acadian dish with roots in Germany and Belgium, uses grated raw potatoes, chicken (variations include beef, shellfish, seafood), salt pork, onions and various seasonings. In pioneer times the gals in the kitchen squeezed the potatoes dry and used potato water as starch for the weekly laundry. When times were lean potatoes alone were used. Molasses is served on the side. Assemble all ingredients before grating the potato.

I admit we cheat with our recipe because we used chicken stock and left over chicken meat. To be authentic, place a cut up chicken in a pot with 4 medium onions (chopped) and water just to cover and boil several hours until meat falls from bones. Separate meat, strain the broth into a bowl and proceed from there. This is a very simple version of Râpure, some folks add seasonings like summer savory and even mashed potatoes and eggs.

meat from one cooked chicken and the strained, reserved stock (see above)
10 large potatoes, peeled
½ pound / 250 g salt pork fat, cut into small cubes
salt and pepper to taste

Cut chicken meat into chunks. Grate potatoes, and put into a cloth bag or large tea towel. Squeeze as much liquid as possible from the potatoes by twisting the bag or cloth tightly over a bowl. Measure the liquid.

Measure out about 2/3 of that amount of broth and bring it to a boil. Add the grated potatoes. Stir together, season with salt and pepper and remove from heat.

In a heavy pot, fry up half of the cubed pork until crisp, mix in the potato mixture. Place half of the potato mixture in a deep casserole dish or rectangular pan, spreading evenly. Cover with chicken meat, then top with the rest of the potato. Sprinkle the remaining salt pork over the top. Bake at 350 degrees F / 180 C, for 1 ½ - 2 hours, depending on the thickness. Serves 6-8

CRISPY POTATO PIE a.k.a. POMMES ANNA

Layer butter, potato slices, and onions in a pie plate. Repeat, topping with butter. Place in the oven, with a plate, and a weight on top and bake until fork tender. To serve, place a larger plate over the pie plate and invert. You should get a crisp, brown "pie" to take to the table.

Auntie Seagull talks about

On the Stove Top

Boiling. Frying. Soups

BOIL 'EM

Probably the most popular way to cook potatoes, boiling is simple, easy and fast. The big question is often to peel or not to peel. Cooking before peeling is said to increase flavour and preserve more nutrients. However, you will have to let them cool a little before peeling after cooking if you don't like the peel going to the table. You might find them easier to peel if you drain, then put in a hot oven to dry. Cool before attempting to peel so that you don't burn your hands.

The one type of potatoes that should always be boiled with skins on, is the tiny, new potato. They are too darn fiddly to peel, and the skins are so tender they can go to the table with their jackets on.

TO BOIL POTATOES

To shorten cooking time cut large potatoes in halves or quarters so that all are about equal in size. Place in saucepan and just cover with water. Cover. Bring to a boil over high heat, then reduce to low and simmer until cooked. Time depends on size of potatoes. If you are in a hurry, or plan to make potato salad or otherwise use diced potatoes, dice them before cooking - they will be done in minutes.

Large potatoes take 30 to 40 minutes. Smaller 15-25 minutes. They are done when a fork passes easily into the centre. Drain when done.

Auntie says:
Instead of adding salt, add flavour by using a good beef or chicken stock instead of water. Fresh mint is a wonderful addition to the water when cooking new potatoes - it speaks of early summer. You can also add herbs or lemon peel, or even garlic, even wine or vegetable juice to your cooking water. Experiment to find your signature method.

HODGEPODGE

Every year Islanders eagerly await the arrival of new potatoes. Bite size morsels of flavour, they and other tiny vegetables are gathered from the garden for a traditional Hodgepodge. This is a sign that summer is truly here. Quantities below are just a suggestion - use what ever new veggies are available and cook them starting with those that need the most time so that all are tender at the same time. Don't overcook - colour and flavour will be lost. Best shared with friends as a celebration of all that is new, fresh and green.

> 2 cups / 500 mL small new potatoes
> 1 cup / 250 mL new baby carrots
> 1 cup / 250 mL yellow wax beans
> 1 cup / 250 mL snow peas
> 1 cup / 250 mL new peas, shelled
> 2 slices bacon, optional
> 1 medium onion, coarsely chopped, or several small baby onions
> 1 cup / 250 mL whipping cream (you can substitute low fat sour cream)
> 2 tbsp / 25 mL butter
> pepper to taste
> 1 tbsp / 15 mL chopped fresh parley

In a large saucepan cook vegetables in about 2 cups / 500 mL boiling water until tender, starting with those requiring the longest cooking time. When done drain, reserving 1/4 cup / 50 mL liquid.

In skillet, fry bacon till crisp. Remove; add onion to fat; saute until tender and golden. Pour off most of fat. Add reserved liquid, cream, butter and bacon. Place vegetables into heated serving dish. Pour cream and bacon mixture over vegetables. Sprinkle with parsley and pepper. Serves 6

STEAMING

Contrary to myth some potatoes can be steamed. Choose waxy boiling potatoes like round Kennebec or Red Pontiac for best results. The benefit is that nutrients stay in the potato rather than being thrown out with the boiling water. Again, subtle flavour can be infused by adding ingredients to the water. Place unpeeled potatoes in a steamer basket so that they don't touch the water. Cover and steam 15 to 25 minutes, depending on size.

NEW POTATOES WITH DILL BUTTER
Wash and dry 1 ½ lb / 750 g new potatoes. Steam to tender. Meanwhile beat ½ cup / 125 mL butter till creamy then blend in 2 tbsp / 25 mL minced fresh dill or 1 tbsp / 15 mL dried. Serve butter in individual cups. Serves 4

MASHING

In days past mashed potatoes were pretty classic - heavy cream and butter (about 1/4 cup / 50 mL of each) were added to cooked potatoes (about 4 large) and the whole lot was blended with a potato masher. Then folks wanted them smoother and began whipping the mixture, using a electric mixer, food processor, or pushing the hot potatoes through a ricer. Personally I don't like my potatoes to loose the consistency you get with a hand potato masher - in other words I like some lumps! Today lumpier, or more roughly mashed potatoes are sometimes referred to as 'smashed.'

Auntie says:
Back in 1899 a recipe for Potatoes (to Mash) read: Boil the potatoes, peel them, and break them to paste; then to two pounds of them add a quarter of a pint of milk, a little salt, and two ounces of butter, and stir it all well over the fire. Either serve them in this manner, or place them on the dish in a form, and then brown the top with a salamander, or in scallops.

No matter the consistency mashed potatoes were usually seasoned with salt and pepper and often served with a pat of butter melting on top. Innovative cooks added veggies such as parsnips, carrots, turnips and even cauliflower and mashed the whole lot together.

Many creative twists are given to mashed potatoes. The most common addition is garlic, but just look at some ideas from other folks. Add the following to your mashed potatoes, to taste.

* low-fat yogurt or low-fat ricotta cheese rather than cream and butter - for a healthier version
* cream cheese or sour cream - bump it up by adding onion or celery salt.
* milk and sour cream (about 3 parts milk, 1 part sour cream), butter and about half as much wasabi to taste.
* Cook equal amounts of potato and cauliflower with a large garlic clove. (1 pound / 500 g cauliflower and potatoes, one clove garlic) mix with small amount of sour cream and snipped fresh chives
* Grate in a favourite cheese (cheddar, Monterey Jack, Blue, Parmesan, etc)
* Fresh herbs such as chopped chives, basil, thyme, marjoram
* Crisp bacon crumbled. Also nice with grated cheese
* Cooked onions, browned in butter, then stirred into the potatoes.
* Diced green, yellow and red peppers look great and taste good. For a bite, go for green chilies or jalapeno peppers. Make special by serving with a bowl of shredded cheese on the side.
* Caraway seeds are a great addition as are sesame, or even sunflower seeds.
* Chopped pickles or relish. Or perhaps your taste is for olives. A great use for those broken ones that cost less money
* Cooked sausage (crumbled into small piece), small cubes of ham or salami, slices of pepperoni sticks.
* For low-cal mashed, mix with low fat or light mayo dressing, a dash of horseradish, sprinkle of garlic powder and 1-2 tablespoons /15-25 mL water

When protein is added to mashed potatoes, consider adding a complimentary salad for a quick and nutritional meal. For example potatoes laden with cheeses or meats would be perfect with a green salad, tomatoes or steamed green, red or yellow veggies.

Auntie says:

Take a tip from housewives of the past planning ahead to prepare for meals that begin with leftover mashed potatoes: Fish Cakes, Bangers and Mash, Home Fries, Shepherd's Pie and many more. The wise cook thinks ahead cutting down preparation time the next day, and using up leftovers.

Auntie says:
When cooking for a crowd, prepare mashed potatoes with a little more liquid (just a bit). When prepared put them into a warm oven-safe bowl, top with grated cheese and place in the oven to keep warm

LOW-CALORIE GARLIC MASHED POTATOES

2 pounds / 1 kg red potatoes, peeled and cut into chunks
4 large cloves garlic, peeled
3/4 cup / 175 mL low-fat buttermilk
salt and black pepper to taste
2 tbsp / 25 mL chopped fresh chives or other garnish

Place potatoes and garlic in large saucepan with water to cover. Bring to boil over high heat, turn down to simmer, uncovered until fork tender (20-30 minutes). Drain and return to pot to dry. Mash with hand masher, or electric mixer to the consistency you prefer. Add all but chives stirring until blended. Garnish and serve hot. Serves 8

SOUTHWESTERN SMASH
Prepare roughly mashed potatoes using butter and milk. Seed and finely chop a jalapeno pepper (one pepper suites 6-7 potatoes) and mix in. Place in an oven-safe bowl, spread about 2-3 inches / 5-8 cm deep. Cover with grated cheese. Use Monterey Jack, or buy a package of mixed cheese blends. Place under a broiler to melt the cheese until it bubbles or browns.

MAKE AHEAD CREAMY MASHED CASSEROLE
Especially good for company or a crowd as it can be made ahead.

Prepare mashed potatoes using 4 oz sour cream and 3 oz cream cheese for every 3 large baking potatoes*. Mash till light and fluffy, seasoning as desired with minced garlic, salt and pepper. Put in a well buttered shallow baking dish, dot with butter and a sprinkle of paprika. Refrigerate until ready to cook. Cover and bake 50 minutes at 400 degrees F / 200 C (25 min if not refrigerated), uncover and bake to golden brown, about 10 more minutes.
* *3 large potatoes serves 4-5 so increase accordingly*

SKILLET MEALS

CODFISH CAKES

Years ago housewives would cook up and mash huge pots of potatoes, far more than could be used at one meal. At the same time a large fillet of salt fish would be put to soak overnight. Changes of water would ensure that the salt was removed and the fish became soft and tender to eat. With no refrigeration fish that had been salted and dried was an important foodstuff because it kept so well, as did potatoes. Serve with chow, a preserved green tomato pickle, and baked beans for a perfect lunch or dinner. Codfish cakes are also popular for breakfast when topped with eggs. Today many replace the traditional chow with ketchup.

    6-8 cups / 1,500-2,000 mL potatoes, mashed with butter and milk
    butter (or oil) for frying
    2 eggs, beaten
1 lb / 500 g salt codfish, freshened and cooked by simmering till tender*
    salt and pepper to taste
    1/4 cup / 50 mL grated raw onion, optional

salt fish is freshened by soaking in cold water to remove some of the salt

Add eggs to mashed potatoes along with fish, salt, pepper and onions. Stir until all is blended well. Shape into cakes. Fry until crusty and brown on both sides. Serve with chow. Serves 4-6

MINI POTATOES WITH CARAMELIZED RED ONIONS

    2 lbs (1kg) mini red potatoes, cut in half, cooked till tender and drained
    1 tbsp (15 mL) olive oil
    ½ cup (125 mL) sliced red onion
    salt and pepper, to taste
    2-3 tbsp (45 mL) balsamic vinegar
    chopped fresh dill

In a skillet, heat oil over medium heat. Add onions. Saute 10-12 minutes or until they turn golden brown (caramelize). Add potatoes, salt and pepper, dill, drizzle with balsamic vinegar and toss gently over low heat until just combined. Garnish with dill sprigs and red onion rings if desired. Serves 6

SALT FISH HASH

We've all heard of Corned Beef Hash, but in many Maritime homes salt fish was much more available. Use Finnan Haddie or salt fish that has been refreshed. With salt fish (even after soaking), add no more salt.

1 cup / 250 mL shredded fish (well shredded and with bones removed)
1 well-beaten egg
2 cups / 500 mL potato cubes
1 tbsp / 15 mL bacon fat (or substitute oil)
pepper
½ tbsp / 10 mL butter

Cook fish and potatoes together until potatoes are tender. Add butter, egg and seasoning. Beat with fork. Melt bacon fat and put fish mixture into hot fat. Spread evenly and cook till a golden brown on bottom. Fold over omelet fashion, serve very hot. Serves 2

CORNED BEEF HASH

Being an English kid I grew up with canned corned beef as a staple in the kitchen. I love it when made into a hash and served with two eggs on top. Some people add an onion to their hash. I didn't but do suggest you try it.

14 oz / 370 g can corned beef or corned beef from deli cut in small cubes
1 pound / 500 g potatoes, cut into small cubes and boiled to tender, or an equal amount of leftover mashed
1 onion, chopped small
2 tbsp / 25 mL Worcestershire sauce
1-2 tsp / 5-10 mL whole grain mustard
2-3 tbsp / 45 mL olive oil (if using canned meat use half this amoutn)
salt and black pepper, to taste
4-8 large eggs

Mix together Worcestershire sauce and mustard in a cup, pour over the corned beef and mix well. Heat oil in a large heavy based frying pan until very hot. Add the onions and toss in the oil for three minutes until well browned. Add the potatoes and toss until browned then season with salt (optional) and pepper. Add the corned beef continuing to toss until everything is hot. In a separate pan fry or poach the eggs. To serve, place eggs on top of hash. Serves 4

FRYING

POTATO PATTIES

An old favourite made in farm kitchens and fried in lard. Today we choose a healthier oil, and probably loose a little flavour in the process. However, realistically speaking, our taste has changed and the lard probably wouldn't be as delicious as our memories try to convince us. The size of the grater, and grating vs shredding dictate whether these have the consistency of a pancake, or a patty

1 egg
1 cup / 250 mL flour
2 cups / 500 mL milk
6 medium potatoes, peeled and grated
1/4 cup / 50 mL oil for cooking

Whisk together egg, flour and milk until well blended. Add the potato slowly, stirring well. The mixture should be smooth. Pour a little of the oil into a frying pan and heat. Pour in batter to make the desired size patty. Fry until brown and crisp on both sides. Serves 4-6

HOME FRIES

There is no question that the best home fries are made in a cast-iron frypan that has been carefully seasoned and maintained. Next best is a grill like those used in restaurants. They just seem to give a better browning power to things like home fries. My mother-in-law used to make great home fries, browned to a crisp and full of flavour. Her secret was to slow cook leftover potatoes over a low-medium heat, not turning them until they had a lovely browned crust on the bottom.

Home fries, to my mind, are not those deep fried frozen things served up in restaurants, They start with good left-overs, just like Auntie Seagull used to make.

Auntie says:

For the very best flavour, and satisfaction for all at the table, heat the plates to hold meals like hash, home fries, etc. Just pop them in the oven for a few minutes.

HOME FRIES

Traditionally made with left over potatoes, however you can start from scratch by peeling and dicing potatoes and boiling until fork-tender.

>4 medium potatoes, cooked and diced
>1/4 cup / 50 mL oil
>4 slices bacon, diced
>1 onion, diced (use a cooking onion or 2-3 green onions, sliced)
>8 mushrooms, sliced, optional
>cooking oil

Use a heavy bottom fry pan. Heat a small amount of oil - just to coat the pan and stop sticking. Add bacon and onion, gently fry until browned. Add mushrooms partway through cooking. Remove and place on paper towels to drain while you cook the potatoes, adding oil if needed. When browned add back the onion mixture and stir to mix well. Serves 6

PARSNIP 'N' POTATO HOME FRIES

Equal amounts of left over parsnips and potatoes and some chopped onion, pan fried in butter or margarine until golden brown, crispy and hot. Season with salt, pepper and paprika to taste.

MUSHROOM AND PEPPER HOME FRIES

Add sliced or chopped mushrooms and green, red or yellow peppers to left-over mashed potatoes and cook as above

BUBBLE AND SQUEAK

The English version of home fries was often made with the left over veggies from Sunday dinner. In our house that meant potatoes, brussels, onions, carrots - whatever veggies were left-over gently fried in drippings or oil until browned. The name Bubble and Squeak comes from the sound this concoction makes as it cooks in a cast iron pan. Bubble and Squeak would be served with left over roast and gravy or with eggs for breakfast.

ACADIAN POTATO PANCAKES

Finely grate 6 potatoes, and mix with 1/4 cup / 50 mL flour, salt and pepper. An egg may be added to bind if you choose. Form into small pancakes about a half inch thick. and fry in hot fat until brown and crisp.

FAIRY LIKE POTATO PUFFS

1 cup / 250 mL mashed potatoes
2 tbsp / 30 mL melted butter
1 cup / 250 mL milk
2 eggs
1/4 cup / 50 mL flour
1 tsp / 5 mL baking powder
1 tsp / 5 mL salt
1/8 tsp / 0.5 mL pepper

Beat mashed potatoes very light with butter and milk; sift in flour, baking powder and seasonings; add well beaten egg yolks and fold in stiffly beaten whites. Drop off a spoon into deep, hot fat. Fry until delicately brown.

POTATO OMELETTE

The secret to this omelette is to dice the potatoes into small cubes. Try using Yukon Gold for a nice flavour and texture.

2 tbsp / 30 mL olive oil
3/4 cup / 175 mL chopped onion
4 cups / 1 L peeled and diced potatoes
6 eggs
salt, optional
sprinkle chopped parsley to garnish

Heat oil in a large skillet over medium heat. Add onion, stir cook about 3 minutes then add potatoes. Cook until tender and golden, about 8 minutes. Meanwhile, whisk eggs in a large bowl and stir in the potatoes. Pour into the skillet over medium heat, cooking about 1 minute before reducing heat to low. Cook until the eggs are set in the centre and lightly browned on the bottom. Slide onto a plate, invert skillet over omelette and flip to turn the omelette. (Or use a second plate on top, invert and slide uncooked side down back into skillet.) Continue cooking just enough to brown the bottom. Cut into wedges, sprinkle with parsley. Serves 6

MEXICAN POTATO OMELETTE

Add a ½ cup / 125 mL of finely chopped red and/or green pepper to the above omelette, and serve with hot sauce or tomato sauce.

> **Auntie says:**
> An electric deep fryer, or a proper cooking pot with a frying basket are best for cooking French fries. A wok or other deep pot can be used but be very careful to allow room for fat to boil up when fries are lowered into the oil.

FRENCH FRIES or CHIPS

The following recipes dating back to the late 1800s may well have been the earliest French Fries and/or potato chips - at least in North America. There is another school of thought that has the French Fry being created in France as a favourite food of the aristocrates. Doesn't matter who was first. We just want to perfect our own recipe!

Saratoga Potatoes
The ingredients speak to the past: potatoes, boiling lard and salt. Peel, and slice on a slaw cutter into cold water, wash throughly and drain; spread between the folds of a clean cloth, rub and pat until dry. Fry a few at a time in boiling lard, salt as you take them out. Saratoga potatoes are often eaten cold. They can be prepared three or four hours before needed, and if kept in a warm place they will be crisp and nice.

Potato Chips
Ingredients: potatoes, boiling lard and salt. Peel a raw potato as apples are peeled, let the parings be as nearly as possible the same thickness, and let them be as long as possible. Dry them thoroughly in a cloth, put them in the frying basket, and plunge it into boiling hot lard. When the chips are a golden colour drain them well in front of the fire, sprinkle a fine salt over them.

> **Auntie says:**
> Today we all know that boiling lard is not healthy. In fact most of us don't even have it in the house. Instead we use healthy cooking oils, and even oven bake our fries

FRENCH FRIES

Use a guide of 1 ½ potatoes per person, depending on the size of the potato. Note that the very best way to make French Fries from scratch means taking several steps. Peeled and cut potatoes must be chilled in ice water for 15 minutes to 2 hours, drained and dried. The longer the chill time, the better. Then they should be fried in two steps: blanching and finishing. This is how the pros do it - my Mom cooked in a wonderful fish and chip shop for years!

> Potatoes, washed, peeled and cut into strips
> oil for deep drying
> accompaniments (ketchup, malt vinegar, salt, pepper or sauce)

To make perfect French fries
* Heat oil to 375 degrees F / 190 degrees C
* Drain and dry potato strips by blotting well on tea towels or paper towels.
* Test temperature of fat by sliding one fry into the oil. It should bubble up when ready
* Put potato strips into frying basket and carefully lower into the hot oil for 6-8 minutes.
*Remove fries, and place on paper towels to drain. These blanched potatoes can be set aside for up to three hours. Refrigerate until needed. This allows advanced preparation.
* Have the rest of the meal ready so that you can serve them at once.
* Heat oil to 400 degrees F / 200 degrees C
* Cook fries in basket 3-5 minutes, until browned and crisp. Drain on paper towels and serve.

STEFAN'S DIPPING SAUCE FOR FRENCH FRIES

Serve crispy French Fries in a basket, with this dipping sauce instead of ketchup or vinegar. This is based on an experience I had in Paris.

> 1 cup sour cream
> 1/4 cup / 50 mL mayo (less if using Miracle Whip)
> 1 tsp / 5 mL mustard powder or 1 tbsp / 15 mL Dijon
> 4 cloves garlic, minced
> 1/4 tsp / 1 mL fresh chopped dill

Mix garlic into mayo then combine all except the dill, use it to garnish.

SOUPS AND CHOWDERS

Soups and chowders have been mainstays in Island homes since the days when wood stoves provided not only a heat source, but a cooking mode that lent itself to one pot meals that could be kept warm till the men of the household came in from the barn or from the wharf after a hard day on the sea. These comfort foods warm the weary, are nutritional, and can be made with just a few basic ingredients found right at home.

FISH CHOWDER

In a chowder pot brown 1 medium chopped onion and ½ cup / 125 mL chopped celery in butter or olive oil. Add 2 cups / 500 mL diced potatoes, ½ cup / 125 mL sliced carrots, salt and pepper to taste, and 2 cups / 500 mL boiling water. Cook till tender. Add a pound or so of fish cut into pieces (white fish or salmon, fresh or frozen). Simmer about 10 minutes. Add 2 cups / 500 mL hot milk and heat without boiling. Serve with tea biscuits or rolls to soak up the juices.

POTATO AND CORN CHOWDER

Quick, easy and delicious. In our house we cut left over corn niblets from cobs that don't get eaten, freeze in small bags and add to this recipe.

1 ½ cups / 375 mL potatoes, peeled and cubed
1 ½ cups / 375 mL chicken stock
1 onion, chopped
3 tbsp / 50 mL butter
2 cups / 500 mL milk
1 large carrot, chopped
½ cups / 125 mL chopped celery, including tops
1 ½ tbsp / 25 mL flour
1 can (14 oz / 397 g) creamed corn + a handful niblets
1 garlic clove, chopped fine, optional

Cook potatoes and carrots in stock 10 minutes, or until tender. Saute onions, garlic and celery in butter 5 minutes. Add flour to onion and blend well. Cook until bubbly. Drain potatoes, saving liquid. Stir milk and potato water into thickened onion mixture. Bring to a boil, stirring constantly. Boil and stir 1 minute. Add corn and vegetables (add additional corn niblets - thawed, if desired). Heat through. Serves 4-6

POTATO LEEK SOUP

This soup is a household favourite because it doesn't use milk or cream. We prefer the taste of a good stock and usually make our own. If none is on hand, buy an organic free-range stock and reduce or eliminate the salt. Potatoes and leeks are natural partners, often used to make a cold pureed soup in Europe. We like it hot and chunky, occasionally adding left over chicken.

> 3 tbsp / 45 mL butter or margarine
> 2 large leeks, sliced (reserve
> 1 large garlic clove, minced
> 1 pound / 500 g potatoes, peeled and cut into large dice
> 3 ½ cups / 875 mL chicken broth
> sea salt to taste
> black pepper to taste

In a good soup or stock pot melt the butter over medium heat. Add leeks and garlic, stirring for 5 minutes. Add the potatoes, chicken broth, salt and pepper. Bring to a boil over high heat. Bring down to a simmer, cover and cook until potatoes are tender. Serves 4

POTATO SOUP

> 1 cup / 250 mL diced potatoes
> 1 small onion
> 2 cups / 500 mL milk
> a little sliced celery
> 1 level tbsp / 15 mL flour
> 1 ½ tsp / 7 mL butter

Cook potatoes, onion and celery in as little water as possible. Add a little to the pulp. Brown flour in butter. Add remainder of the milk and cook until thickened a little. Add to pulp mixture and season to taste. Pour soup over small amount of breadcrumbs. Serves 2

Auntie says:
One pound of white potatoes, generally equals 3 medium. Chopped or sliced that will measure 3 ½ to 4 cups. Cooked and mashed, it will be approximately 1 3/4 cups.

ACADIAN POTATO SOUP

Similar to the previous Anglophone version. Acadians made a soup by boiling and mashing potatoes, then adding a second onion that has been browned in butter which gave a great flavour. This recipe came from a lovely lady "up west" who was known for the delicious meals she served up using basic local ingredients. A real old-fashioned housewife who gave me an introduction to Acadian cooking.

3 large potatoes, peeled and cut in 6
2 large onions, peeled and chopped
butter
flour
3 ½ cups / 875 mL milk
salt and pepper to taste
dried herbs such as summer savory, parsley or chives

Boil potatoes and half of the onion until tender. While cooking fry the remaining onion in a lump of butter (about 2 tbsp / 25 mL) until browned, then stir in 1 tbsp / 15 mL of flour until a paste forms. Slowly add milk stirring until thick and heated through. Reduce heat so that it doesn't boil.

Drain the potatoes (reserving a cup of cooking liquid) mash and add to sauce. Blend in some of the potato cooking water, stirring until the consistency you want for your soup. Season with salt and pepper to taste and return to a low heat until all is hot. To serve add a sprinkle of herbs and a pat of butter. Serves 4

MINTY NEW POTATO SOUP

This dish is generally served as a soup today, but long ago, when food was not as plentiful or varied, it was a main course.

Scrape small new potatoes and turn into an oven-proofed dish. Cover with milk and season with salt and pepper. Add a large quantity of mint sprays or leaves, enough to give the mint flavour you desire. Bring to a boil and simmer gently for 15-20 minutes. Take care that the milk doesn't boil over (Do Not put the lid on tight!).

Auntie Seagull talks about

Other Stuff

Salads.Breads.Cakes.Candy

SALADS

Potatoes and summer salads go hand in hand in Prince Edward Island. Deemed a perfect make-ahead addition to a picnic or barbecue they tend to take on the persona of the individual who makes them. Most need to be made and refrigerated for several hours to obtain the best flavour.

BASIC POTATO SALAD

>6 medium potatoes, boiled with skins on
>1 onion, chopped
>4 hard-boiled eggs, peeled and sliced
>1 cup / 250 mL chopped celery
>1 tsp / 5 mL salt
>½ cup / 125 mL salad dressing or mayonnaise

Peel potatoes and dice. Reserve 8 center slices of egg, then roughly chop the remainder. When potatoes are cool combine with other ingredients. Place in a nice bowl, garnish with egg slices and chill for at least 4 hours. Serves 8

POTATO SALAD WITH CRUNCH
To zip up your potato salad add diced green or red pepper, sliced radish, sunflower seeds, pine nuts and a little more dressing - all to taste.

STEFAN'S POTATO SALAD
You can almost always tell a chef's recipe by the number of ingredients and the care that goes into preparation. Their skills really show with all the dicing in this recipe.

    4 tbsp / 60 mL Miracle Whip or home made dressing
    1 tbsp / 15 mL dijon mustard
    1 tbsp / 15 mL sour cream
    3 radishes, diced small
    1 pickle, diced small
    1/4 cup / 50 mL each of red, yellow and green peppers, diced
    1/3 cup / 75 mL corn niblets
    ½ carrot, diced small
    10 - 12 chives, chopped
    1 tomato, diced small
    2 strips cooked bacon, crumbled
    2 shallots, diced small
    5 Yukon Gold potatoes, cooked, peeled and diced
    1 lemon juiced
    pepper and salt, to taste

Combine all ingredients until evenly distributed. Place in serving bowl, garnish with paprika and refrigerate until ready to be served. Serves 4-6

PEA, PIMENTO, POTATO SALAD
Another traditional potato salad always contained peas. In days past they were often canned. Today we have the luxury of thawing frozen peas for a fresh from the garden taste.

    2 ½ pounds / 1,250 g white potatoes, peeled, diced and boiled fork-tender
    2 tbsp / 25 mL white vinegar
    1 jar (6 oz / 180 mL) sliced pimentos, drained and chopped
    1 cup / 250 mL sweet peas
    2 green onions, sliced
    mayonnaise to bind salad

Drain potatoes, returning them to the hot pot to dry; sprinkle with vinegar. When cool, transfer to a bowl and add the pimentos, onion and peas. Stir in just enough mayo to bind, season with salt and pepper if desired. Serves 6

WARM GOURMET POTATO SALAD

Another family favourite. When planning a good feed of steamed mussels, we strive to have a few left for the next day. Shuck meats into glass jars or bowls, cover and refrigerate. Strain and reserve liquid, freezing leftovers for future use. Meats are great fried, or used in a potato salad.

4 cups / 1,000 mL diced boiled potatoes
2 cups / 500 mL mussel meats
2 tbsp / 30 mL chopped parsley
2 tbsp / 30 mL chopped chives or green onion tops
2 tbsp / 30 mL chopped shallots of green onion
1 tsp / 5 mL celery seed
½ cup / 125 mL mussel broth or bottled clam juice
½ cup / 125 mL white vinegar
2 tsp / 10 mL sugar
½ tsp / 2 mL Dijon-style mustard
salt to taste
pimiento strips, or slivers of red pepper, for garnish

In a bowl combine potatoes, mussels, parsley, chives, shallots and celery seed. In saucepan combine broth, vinegar, sugar and mustard; heat just to boiling and pour over salad. Toss, adding salt to taste. Serve while still warm with garnish. Serves 4

Auntie says:

If your soup is too thin add mashed potatoes, stirring until you get the desired consistency.

If soup or stew is too salty when preparing, add a few slices of raw potato. Discard the potato before serving.

When boiling potatoes, save the leftover cooking water instead of pouring it down the sink. It is great to use in gravy, soups, stews and even in baked goods

BREADS AND SWEET TREATS

Almost always at hand, potatoes made their way into a number of unexpected dishes particularly baked goods such as bread, biscuits, cakes, pies and even candy. Potato Bread has a texture that keeps it popular with those who savour traditional foods. Many of these recipes came from eras when food was scarce, or the money to buy many ingredients was hard to come by.

POTATO BREAD
This recipe from the kitchens of Chef Stefan Czapalay's book, Seasons In Thyme will confirm that there are few things nicer than a slice of fresh, or toasted, potato bread.

> 18 oz / 511 g potatoes (3 medium Russets)
> 1 1/4 cups / 300 mL water
> 1 1/4 cups / 300 mL milk
> 4 tbsp / 60 mL (4 pkg) yeast
> 2 1/4 lb / 1,125 g semolina flour
> 2 tsp / 10 mL salt
> ½ tsp / 2 mL nutmeg

Cook and mash the potatoes and cool a bit. Combine water and milk. Dissolve the yeast in 6 tbsp water/milk mixture. Sift flour and salt together in a bowl, and knead in the nutmeg and potatoes. Smooth; add yeast and liquid, and knead. Cover and proof for 2 hours until double in size. Knead, shape and proof for 30 minutes more; place in a greased pan, covered with a damp cloth. Bake at 425 degrees F / 220 C for 45 minutes. Remove from oven, turn out and place on rack to cool. Makes one loaf.

Auntie says:
When making a recipe with bulk ingredients such as the semolina flour above, it is a good idea to take the recipe to a bulk store and measure out the exact quantity right at the store where they have scales. Makes life so much easier!.

POTATO BISCUIT

1 cup / 250 mL mashed potato
1 cup / 250 mL flour
3 tsp / 15 mL baking powder
1 tsp / 5 mL salt
2 tbsp / 30 mL fat
2/3 cup / 150 mL water or milk (about)

Sift together flour, baking powder and salt. Work in the fat with a fork or knife. Add potato and mix thoroughly. Then add enough liquid to make a soft dough. Roll the dough lightly to about ½ inch / 1 ½ cmin thickness. Cut into biscuits. Bake 13 to 15 minutes in hot oven (400 degrees F / 200 C)

Auntie says:
In days gone by innovative Mom's would place large potatoes in the oven an hour or so before bedtime. Then, the potatoes would be placed in a thick wool sock, to make a perfect bed warmer.

POTATO STUFFING

8 large potatoes, boiled
1/4 cup / 50 mL milk
4 tbsp / 60 mL butter
5 cups / 1,250 mL dried bread cubes
2 eggs
1 large onion, chopped fine
3/4 cup / 175 mL diced celery
1 tsp / 5 mL salt
1 tsp / 5 mL poultry seasoning
black pepper
2 tbsp / 25 mL finely chopped chives

Drain boiled potatoes and mash with butter and milk. Cool. Soak the bread cubes in cold water and squeeze excess moisture out. Beat the eggs and stir them and all other ingredients into potatoes until all blended. Use to stuff a turkey or large chicken.

POTATO DOUGHNUTS

Doughnuts were very popular in the 1890s and many old handwritten recipes can be found for them. Easy to make they could be chilled while chores were done. Lard was very common which would increase the popularity.

4 cups / 1,000 mL flour
3 tsp / 15 mL cream of tartar
1 tsp / 5 mL salt
1 cup / 250 mL mashed potatoes
1 1/4 cup / 300 mL sugar
½ cup / 125 mL butter
1 ½ tsp / 7 mL soda
2 tsp / 10 mL nutmeg
2/3 cup / 150 mL milk
3 eggs
½ tsp / 2 mL vanilla

Combine flour, soda, cream of tartar, nutmeg and salt. Set aside. Beat milk and potatoes together until smooth. Beat eggs with sugar and melted butter until light. Add vanilla. Blend in dry ingredients gradually, alternating with milk mixture, beginning and ending with dry ingredients. Chill 1 ½ hours. Roll half the dough at a time, chilling the rest. Roll out to 3/8 inch / 2 cm thick. Cut into donut shapes. Fry in fat at 375 degrees F / 190 C until brown, turning once. Drain and set on rack. Dip in sugar if desired.

Auntie says:

To the French, the potato is known as pomme de terre, a phrase meaning: 'apple of the earth' Conversely, French fries are called pommes frites. The name French fries was not given to them because they were invented in France, but rather because the potatoes are 'frenched' - cut into lengthwise strips. Just to complicate matters the English call French fries, chips. North Americans give that name to potato chips which the British know as Crisps.

POTATO CAKE

1/4 cup / 50 mL shortening
2 cups / 500 mL sugar
4 egg yolks
1 cup / 250 mL plain, unseasoned mashed potatoes
2 cups / 500 mL all-purpose flour
1/4 tsp / 1 mL salt
2 tsp / 10 mL baking powder
½ cup / 125 mL milk
2 squares unsweetened chocolate, grated
4 egg whites
1 cup / 250 mL chopped walnuts
1 tsp / 5 mL vanilla

Cream shortening and sugar very well. Beat in egg yolks and mashed potatoes, mixing well. This requires much beating. Sift together flour, salt and baking powder. Add dry ingredients and chocolate alternately with milk to creamed mixture. Add unbeaten egg whites one at a time; beat after each addition. Add walnuts, beating well, add vanilla and beat. Pour into greased and floured rectangular cake pan, about 13 x 9 inches / 32 x 22 cm. Bake in a 350 F / 175 C oven 45 to 50 minutes.

POTATO CHIP COOKIES

1 cup / 250 mL shortening, creamed
1 cup / 250 mL white sugar, added
1 cup / 250 mL brown sugar, added
2 eggs, unbeaten, one at a time
2 cups / 500 mL flour
1 tsp / 5 mL soda
1 tsp / 5 mL vanilla
1 cup / 250 mL crushed potato chips
3/4 cup / 175 mL chopped nuts

Combine shortening and sugars. Add eggs, flour, soda, vanilla. Add chips and nuts last. Makes a stiff dough. Using hand form into balls. Flatten with a fork dipped in hot water. Bake 10-15 minutes in a 350 degree F / 180 degree C oven

MOLASSES DROPS

A staple in Island kitchens molasses appears in many recipes for sweet goods. Not as sweet as refined sugar, it was much more easily available.

>2 cups / 500 mL flour
>½ tsp / 2 mL baking soda
>2 tsp / 10 mL baking powder
>½ tsp / 2 mL ginger
>½ tsp / 2 mL cinnamon
>½ tsp / 2 mL salt
>½ cup / 125 mL dark molasses
>½ cup / 125 mL butter
>1/3 cup / 75 mL brown sugar
>1 ½ cup / 375 mL mashed potatoes
>1 cup / 250 mL chopped walnuts or pecans
>powdered sugar

Preheat oven to 375 degrees F / 190 C. Sift together flour, soda, powder, ginger, cinnamon, and salt. Combine molasses and butter in the top of a double boiler and place over hot water. Beat until heated through and the butter is completely melted. Add dry ingredients and brown sugar. Mix well. Adding a little at a time, beat in the potatoes until all is smooth and well blended. Stir in nuts. Butter a baking sheet and drop batter by the teaspoonful onto it. Bake for 10 minutes. Remove from oven, sprinkle with powdered sugar and allow to cool before eating. About 50 cookies.

Auntie says:
If there is an ongoing theme in this collection of recipes it is, 'waste not, want not.' Cooks used potatoes in recipes such as these, even throwing potato peelings into the soup pot. One collectors recipe had a double crust pie, with a filling of.... you guessed it .... mashed potatoes. Bet they served it with molasses!

POTATO MARZIPAN

First time I had the spud version of Marzipan was at a culinary event where students were challenged to use potato. They fashioned this marzipan into small potato replicas to garnish a potato cake. Follow their example and fashion edible decorations to reflect hobbies, favourite foods or even people. Great fun for holidays like Christmas or Easter. Good for decorations on desserts such as cup cakes, or serve on their own as a delicacy at a tea party or event where small sweets are appropriate. Mix in with chocolates to truly personalize a gift.

½ cup / 125 mL mashed potatoes
½ tsp / 2 mL almond extract
4 ½ cups / 1,125 mL confectioners sugar

In a small bowl beat potatoes and almond extract with an electric mixer on low speed until smooth. Gradually beat in the confectioners sugar to make a stiff dough. Congratulations, you have made potato marzipan. Shape into forms. Traditionally these would be fruits or easy things to replicate. Place on a tray and set aside to dry. Brush with food colourings to make them fun and appealing. Once dry, they can be stored in a covered container for up to a week. Keep in a cool place. Makes 2 cups / 500 mL

POTATO CREAMS

In days past sweet treats such as candy were made at home, and not assembly line products picked up at the checkout. The making was half the fun! Read this recipe carefully before starting. It calls for the addition of flavouring and other ingredients which need to be decided on and gathered.

½ cup / 125 mL hot riced potato
2 cups / 500 mL confectioners sugar
2 cups / 500 mL coconut
1 oz / 28 g chocolate
flavouring extract of your choice
chopped ginger, candied fruit, or nuts

Sift sugar into potato; add a flavouring extract and coconut, chopped ginger; candied fruits or nuts. Mix well and spread in a small cake pan. Melt chocolate and spread on top in a thin layer. When firm cut in squares.

Seacroft

BOOK STORE

Seacroft, is a small publishing house located in Prince Edward Island. We produce a variety of books on several topics: folklore/history, cooking, small business/entrepreneurship, travel, and more. Seacroft even has a line of greeting cards and calendars. Check it all out at

www.seacroftpei.com

There will soon be some new "Auntie Seagull...." books as well!! and she delivers!

To order books from Seacroft check out the list on the next page and for even more topics visit our website at www.seacroftpei.com

To order now send your cheque and full mailing information (name, mailing address, phone number or email) to:

Seacroft
P.O. Box 1204
Charlottetown, PE Canada
C1A 7M8

Want a personalized autograph, just tell us details

COOKBOOKS

Seafood Cookery of Prince Edward Island
$19.95 + $1.00 gst + $5.00 shipping = $25.95

Seafood Menus for the Microwave - Full Course Meals in a Flash
$16.00 + $.80 + $4.00 shipping = $20.80

Simple Pleasures From Our Maritime Kitchens
(winner of the Canadian Food Culture Award from Cuisine Canada)
$20.00 + $1.00 gst + $5.00 shipping = $26.00

Cultured Mussel Cookbook - Pioneering an Industry
Retail Price - $13.95 + $.70 gst + $4.00 shipping = $18.65

Sensational Seafood
$14.95 + $.75 gst + $4.00 shipping = $18.70

Seafood Basics......buying . storing . cleaning . cooking fish and shellfish
$9.95 + .50 gst + $3.50 shipping = $13.95

Potato Basics.......a potpourri of recipes, how to and spud lore from Prince Edward Island
$9.95 + .50 gst + $3.50 shipping = $13.95

For more information about book content, sizes, number of pages etc. go to www.seacroftpei.com